HOUSEPLANTS

Care and Management

HOUSEPLANTS
Care and Management

Christina Payne and Hazel Dodgson

B T BATSFORD LTD. LONDON

Frontispiece:
Cyclamen

First published 1982

ISBN 0 7134 4166 6

Filmset by Servis Filmsetting Ltd, Manchester
and printed in Hong Kong
for the publishers
B T Batsford Ltd
4 Fitzhardinge Street
London W1H 0AH

Contents

Acknowledgments

The authors wish to thank the following for their help in the preparation of this book: Mrs Barbara Harrington for typing the manuscript, Ruxley Manor Nurseries (Sidcup) for their advice and co-operation, Mrs Ilse Sherry, Mrs Hilda Woods, Mrs Carol Robinson, Mrs Bush, Rebecca Homersham, and Charlie Hoddaway.

Plants were provided by Ruxley Manor Nurseries, to whom we are grateful.

All the photographs were provided by Panther Photographic International (H Dodgson and C Payne).

Introduction

This book aims to introduce you to the rewarding and fascinating hobby of keeping and propagating houseplants.

We have chosen varieties that are readily available and easy to grow, giving a wealth of colours, sizes and shapes. The plants are grouped according to the conditions that they like, enabling you to choose the right locations in your own home to suit their needs.

Techniques of propagation are given, which will enable you to maintain a supply of 'free' plants; there are also ideas on arrangement and display.

Common pests and diseases that may attack your houseplants are explained, and advice given on how to maintain your plants successfully.

We hope you will enjoy reading this book and that it will prove to be a useful source of information and help.

1 Plants to Choose and Where to Put Them

Houseplants often do not thrive and sometimes even die because they are not situated in the correct environment. It is really quite a simple matter to give your plants the right conditions provided you know what your own home has to offer – its advantages and limitations. Before you have a trip to the nursery to choose your plants, inspect your house first. Determine where the sunny parts are, in other words the parts of the house which face south and south-west. Easterly and north-easterly-facing windows will not receive as much light and therefore those areas will be darker. Northerly-facing windows will receive an even light, but no direct sun. Shady parts of the house can be lightened if the walls are painted with a pastel shade; and white will offer the maximum reflection and can be used very successfully to lighten a wall that would otherwise be too dark.

Next see how draughty the house is. Plants do not like draughts so inspect closely. Some places are more susceptible than others, for example the bottom of a staircase or the areas behind doors which open to the outside. If your house does not have central heating then you will probably suffer from warm rooms and cold hallways. As soon as the door is opened an icy blast of cold air will rush into the room spelling great danger to any plants in its path. The joints in window frames are another dangerous problem. The air forcing its way through a window frame can be deadly, especially in winter. Double glazing will help, and usually windows so treated are safe.

Maintaining the humidity of the air is vitally important to many plants. Grouping plants helps to maintain humidity, as they create their own local environment. Alternatively, stand them on a tray of moist pebbles or wet sand. Areas such as the bathroom and kitchen often have a high natural level of humidity and provided the rooms are not too dark will prove ideal.

Keeping the temperature constant, without fluctuation, is a difficult problem. Central heating makes this easier but if your house does not have this facility then do not choose to keep plants that will not withstand the temperature fluctuations other forms of heating produce. Your plants at worst will die and at least will not thrive. There are many plants you *can* grow successfully, and which give you a lovely display, so take heart.

Therefore, instead of just describing plants and leaving you to work out where to put your charges, we have grouped plants together according to the conditions that they like.

We begin with plants that enjoy being in direct sunlight for a considerable period of time. This does not mean that they do not like other areas and where they do we will say so. However, plants in the other sections do not like direct sun and therefore should not be exposed to it. The next group will be the plants that like average sunny conditions with some shade offered, and the last group are those which will live happily in very shady conditions. Most of the varieties in this book like to be watered freely in the growing season, without water-logging, and to be kept just moist in the winter. There are a few exceptions and these are mentioned accordingly. Feed all your plants every two weeks in the growing season with a

proprietary houseplant food available from your nursery and re-pot in the spring. Again there are one or two exceptions to the rule.

Plants Which Tolerate Direct Sunlight

Direct sunlight coming through glass can be very damaging to plants. It can cause scorched leaves and wilting because of the higher heat intensity. Few plants like this, but those that are strong enough to withstand the sun's rays will positively thrive. Try to give these plants as much direct sun as possible, at least three hours a day – a little difficult perhaps in Britain!

The family of Bromeliads includes many varieties, one of which is the edible Pineapple Plant, **Ananas**. It has the most decorative foliage with leaves long and slender carrying spines and sharp-toothed edges. The plant flower is carried on a bract which appears in the centre of the plant. The bract is usually pink, the flowers blue.

Ananas are slow growers and need lots of light with a minimum temperature of 18°C (64°F) and high humidity. They like to be fairly dry, so water moderately keeping the compost on the dry side. Clay pots are more suitable than plastic ones which tend to topple over because of the weight of the plant.

With such fastidious requirements it is inadvisable to attempt to keep these if you are a novice as they are extremely difficult to grow. The fruit produced indoors is seldom edible.

A very popular houseplant is the **Beloperone** (Shrimp Plant) and as the name suggests it is covered in salmon-pink bracts with white flowers resembling shrimps. The leaf is palish green and heart-shaped. There are several stems growing from the base and the plant will grow to approximately 14–20in in height. When fully grown and in full bloom the plant is really quite beautiful. Flowers are usually present all year. Its minimum temperature requirement is 7°C (45°F). Spray the leaves occasionally with tepid water.

Tip cuttings can be taken in springtime to produce more Beloperone and in March prune the plant down to the base to promote bushy growth in the summer. As the plant grows pinch out the growing tips to maintain the bushy habit.

A Bromeliad that is very easy to grow is **Bilbergia**. The leaves are sword-shaped and arranged into a tube-shaped rosette. Bilbergias vary in size and shape but the flowers are usually tubular with petals that arch outwards and are backed by papery-looking bracts. Bilbergias may bloom at any time of the year, and therefore do not have a resting period. They grow well in normal temperatures and will withstand a minimum temperature of 7°C (45°F). Water moderately throughout the year to keep the compost just moist. Rain water or lime-free water is best. Bilbergia likes a certain amount of humidity although it is very happy in dry conditions. Propagate by offsets in the spring (see page 31).

Calceolaria (Slipper Flower) is a very colourful plant. Calceolarias like to have high humidity and this is best obtained by standing the plant on a tray of wet pebbles. Their minimum temperature is 7°C (45°F) so most homes will be able to support them.

The leaves on the adult plant are very large, spreading up to 8in across. They are heart-shaped and grouped around the base of a single central stem. Above the leaves rise several branching stalks 1–2ft long which carry loose clusters of slipper-shaped flowers. The flowers, which can be almost any colour, vary in size from $\frac{1}{2}$in to 2in across. The orange, yellow and reddish-brown flowers tend to be seen most frequently and they have lovely blotches of contrasting colour on them. After flowering the plants are discarded.

Use the Calceolaria to add lots of colour to your other houseplants and do not forget to include them in larger displays.

Capsicum, the Pepper Plant, possesses lovely profuse fleshy fruit which form in the winter. They are bushy plants and low-growing, reaching a height of 18in. The stems are woody and the leaves

Left:
Ananas with fruit

Right:
**Beloperone showing
its characteristic
'shrimps'**

lance-shaped. The fruit when formed remain decorative for 8–12 weeks, after which time they wrinkle and fall off. The plants require a minimum temperature of 10°C (50°F) and prefer a little humidity.

Capsicums are very easy to grow and give a fine display of colour in the drab winter months. As soon as the fruits have gone discard the plants. New plants are raised from seed and this is best left to the nurseryman.

Chlorophytum (Spider Plant) is one of the most popular houseplants and one that is very easy to grow. The leaves are slender green with a white stripe. The leaves arch when at their full length giving a cascade of unsurpassed beauty. In summer appearing through the foliage will grow a stem that may reach to 2ft. This will bear little white flowers and from these will grow tiny plantlets or 'spiders' which resemble the adult plant. The plantlets can be left attached to the main plant and will thrive and continue to grow, or can be transplanted to produce new individuals. With its plantlets and

The beautiful Bilbergia flower

arching leaves, Chlorophytum makes an ideal specimen for a hanging basket. It can attain a height of 10in and requires a minimum temperature of 7°C (45°F).

Chrysanthemums are well known and very popular but are not really true houseplants. They are kept indoors only for the flowering period after which time they should either be discarded or planted in the garden. Potted Chrysanthemums are now available in flower at any time of year which makes them ideal to add colour and sparkle in your home. The height of the potted types is about 18in. They do not grow any higher because the growing tips have been pinched out. They are usually nice and bushy with a wealth of flower buds. When choosing one however, avoid those with tightly closed green buds as these often fail to open. To achieve maximum flowering, give the plant at least three hours direct sunlight a day. They are very tolerant and do not object to draughts. They will take a minimum temperature of 10°C (50°F).

Cineraria are best regarded as 'temporary' houseplants, brought in when flowering to give lots of colour. Although direct sunlight is appreciated, they must be kept cool otherwise the plant will wilt; similarly if the compost dries out the plant will collapse.

Flowers appear in late winter, and early spring, providing colour at a difficult time of year. After flowering they should be planted outdoors or discarded.

Although **Clivia** like direct sunlight, do not leave them all day in direct sun. Mid-day sun will scorch the leaves. They develop into impressive plants. They must have a winter rest in a cool and shady place to ensure a healthy display the following year. Their leaves are dark green, and fan out from the base which is layered in leaf bases. Clivia produces a fine orange or red flower which appears in the winter. The flower stalk may reach a height of 18in. Direct sun is needed to obtain the flowers. Rest the plants in early winter at a temperature of 10°C (50°F) for about eight weeks. Transfer them

to a warm room where the temperature should be as high as possible. Keep the plant almost dry in the winter.

Codiaeums, otherwise known as crotons, are bushy shrubs that can grow to 3ft high. They have smooth leathery leaves on short stalks. The colour varies from green to orange and red with yellow veins. Propagate in the spring with tip cuttings. Do not allow the temperature to fall below 10°C (50°F) otherwise the leaves will drop off.

Coleus are usually regarded as temporary foliage plants and discarded when they are past their best. The leaves are most attractive and can be found in almost any colour. They usually have a low habit and therefore are ideal to put amongst plant displays to give added colour. If they are not given really bright light then the leaves will become spindly. They need a high humidity and a warm room, about 18°C (65°F). They will withstand a drop of temperature to 13°C (53°F) but below this the leaves will fall off. Water plentifully and do not allow the compost to dry out otherwise the leaves will collapse. Re-pot every three months. The habit should remain bushy so pinch out the growing tips regularly. Coleus are not recommended for the beginner as they are fastidious in their requirements.

A Bromeliad with a low growing habit is **Cryptanthus** (Earth Star). It produces star-shaped rosettes of leaves that are tough and pointed with prickly edges. The leaves can be plain or striped and covered with a bloom. They like a humid environment with a warm temperature although in the winter will tolerate a minimum temperature of 10°C (50°F). Water sparingly at all times to keep the compost barely moist. They do not require much feeding – usually once a month is adequate. When re-potting use a peat-based compost although re-potting is rarely necessary. Offsets are produced in springtime, which may be propagated (see page 44). The plant is quite difficult to grow and is often killed by over-watering.

Solanum (Winter Cherry) makes a lovely

An attractively
displayed
Chlorophytum
showing several
plantlets

Several varieties of Codiaeums

it standing on a cold windowsill. Keep the compost thoroughly moist but do not stand the plant in water. You can keep the plant for a second season but when fruiting has finished let it rest and, if possible, put it outside. During the resting period keep the compost only just moist; re-potting can be carried out during this time. After the first season prune to half of the original size. This will ensure a bushy plant for the second season.

Vallota is an excellent plant for a sunny window, producing lovely trumpet flowers in clusters in late summer. The flowers are carried on a single tall stem. Normal room temperatures are fine but avoid drastic temperature fluctuations. It will withstand a minimum temperature of 10°C (50°F) when it is resting in the winter. Water sparingly, just enough to keep the compost moist. It prefers a rich soil-based potting mixture. Vallota may be propagated by division in the spring or early summer (see page 49).

Yucca has only recently become a popular houseplant. The plants have short brown trunk-like stems which sprout clusters of long leathery leaves. Flowers are not likely on Yuccas grown indoors. A wide range of temperatures can be tolerated, and the plants are happy at 10°C (50°F) in the winter. They enjoy dry air and will thrive in conditions not liked by other plants. Re-pot in the spring. Due to the size and weight of these plants it is best to use clay pots. Yuccas benefit from being stood outside during the summer months when they will produce more growth. If this is not possible however, do not worry because they will still be happy indoors. Yuccas can grow quite tall, so they make ideal subjects to put at the rear of a display.

Group plants according to their humidity requirements. Most plants liking direct sun do not mind dry air but remember that Beloperone, Bilbergia, Capsicum, Chlorophytum and Coleus prefer a high humidity. If you are thinking of displaying your plants together, keep these separate from the other types mentioned in this group that like the air dry.

houseplant, giving a profusion of bright orange fruit in the winter. Solanum will want a high humidity and frequent spraying of the leaves with water. Frost will kill, so make sure you do not leave

15

Left:
**The attractive
leaves of Coleus**

Right:
Cryptanthus

Plants Requiring Moderate Sun and Shade

The second group of plants all like to have sunny conditions and a little shade, but do not like direct sunlight. The group includes types that like a high humidity and others which do not mind the air dry. Most of them are easy to grow although we have included a few more difficult ones for those of you who feel more ambitious.

There is plenty of scope with these varieties for increasing their numbers as most can easily be propagated.

All those plants which like direct sunlight, and which have already been described, may also be included in this group, so do not forget to include them in your displays and arrangements.

No plants like draughts, so remember this important aspect of plant care when you are siting your charges.

The most popular and one of the prettiest of the pot-grown ferns is the **Adiantum** (Maiden Hair Fern). The leafstalks resemble human hair and the fronds are 15in long. Spores are produced on the undersides of the pinnae. They grow well in normal room temperatures and can tolerate temperatures of 10°C (50°F). If they get too hot (24°C, 75°F) spray the plants and stand them on moist pebbles to raise the humidity.

The plant will die if the roots dry out, but water only sufficiently to keep the compost permanently moist. Feed occasionally during the growing season.

Propagate them by taking sections of the rhizome with fronds attached in spring. Use a peat-based compost.

Aechmea (Urn Plant) is a Bromeliad and quite difficult to grow, requiring a minimum temperature of 17°C (63°F). The leaves are very tough with spines on the edges, clasped together in a rosette. In the centre is a cup to catch water and this should not be allowed to dry out, and from it the flower stalk appears with a pink stem carrying small blue flowers. As it flowers only when mature, it is best to purchase the plant already in 'bloom'. Keep the humidity high and constant throughout the year. Stand on a tray of moist pebbles. Aechmeas can withstand short periods of cold reasonably well. Water moderately and use only rainwater to fill the cup.

Happy in bright light, the **Aphelandra** (Saffron Spike) grows to 12–18in and has stout stems with dark, glossy, pointed green leaves. In spring yellow spikes are produced on a bract. The colour does not last long but the cone-shaped bract remains for several weeks. They are not easy to bring into bloom however and it is best to purchase one already in flower. The humidity needs to be high but the plant will withstand a minimum temperature of 10°C (50°F) in the winter. Cuttings can be taken in spring. Water plentifully in the summer but keep the compost fairly dry in the resting period. Feeding must be done every week as these are terribly greedy plants. This plant often dies on people mainly because the summer temperature of 18°C (65°F) cannot always be maintained easily. Not a good choice for a beginner but a lovely plant to have when you have acquired some experience.

Asparagus, not the type you eat but a very popular houseplant, is very easy to grow. It will tolerate most things and is happy in a minimum temperature of 7°C (45°F). Asparagus will benefit from a lot of humidity but does not seem to mind dry conditions. The plants look like ferns with plume-like fronds growing from a central crown. The flowers are small but do exude some fragrance. After flowering a plant will produce red or orange berries. After three years divide the plant and replant the sections. Asparagus looks lovely in a hanging basket.

As the English name suggests, the **Aspidistra** (Cast Iron Plant) is extremely tolerant of abuse, but responds very well to good care. The leaves are dark green and leathery, 15–20in long. The flowers are insignificant.

The plant is so tolerant that it will flourish in hot and cold rooms, withstanding a minimum temperature of 7°C (45°F). Water moderately to make

the compost barely moist. Overwatering will produce brown marks on the leaf surface. Propagate by dividing clumps in spring.

Begonia consists of many varieties and has dark-green leaves with an abundance of flowers in vivid colours, pinks, reds, yellow, and oranges which almost fluoresce at you because they are so bright. The flower types also vary, from enormous blooms which seem too heavy for the stem to tiny almost daisy-like varieties. They dislike dry conditions and require a high humidity. Be careful not to let water settle on the leaves as this will cause mildew. The Begonia likes a good natural light but dislikes direct sunlight and needs to be draught free. Feed once a week when flowering and water freely. Always remove any dead flowers, at the same time checking for mildew. It is best for the plant's sake to maintain a steady warmth although the minimum temperature can go as low as 10°C (50°F). Begonias are corms and need re-potting annually. In the winter they will become dormant but do not let them come into contact with frost as this will kill them. Properly cared for they will give you an endless supply of colour throughout the summer.

There are other types of Begonia grown just for the colour and texture of the leaves. Known as *Begonia Rex* they require the same conditions as their relatives and look marvellous when grouped with the flowering types.

Campanula (Star of Bethlehem) is very easy to grow, with beautiful star-shaped blue flowers on the stem which trail. The leaves are bright green, heart-shaped and tooth-edged. The leaf is also rather brittle. Should the stem be broken sap will come out. This is white with a slight odour, which is not unpleasant. The plant is ideal for hanging baskets as the trails can reach one foot in length. The flowers are at their best in midsummer. The Campanula needs a cool position in summer although it needs lots of light. A north facing window would be ideal. It will withstand a minimum temperature of 7°C (45°F). Propagate by taking tip cuttings. The plant likes a high

Aphelandra showing its distinctive ivory-white marking

Right:
The flower of the Begonia with striking leaves of the Begonia Rex

humidity but watch carefully for signs of grey mould infection.

Best treated as a 'temporary' houseplant, the **Cyclamen** produces the most beautiful flowers in vivid colours during the winter months. The Cyclamen prefers a cool position although it hates draughts. If too hot the flowers will drop. Do not water the plant from the top but stand it in a bowl of water. When the compost is moist remove the plant and place back into its original position. Remove dead flowers and stalks as soon as they appear. Frost will kill the plant, so do not put it near a window at night. Cyclamen are best discarded when they have finished flowering as it is very difficult to produce vigorous growth and flowers in the following growing season.

Cyperus (Umbrella Sedge) thrives in very moist conditions; it has thin rust-like unjointed stems, topped with narrow leaf-like bracts, with brown or greenish grass-like flower heads. The height is approximately 18in and some can grow to as much as 8ft. So be careful which you choose! Minimum temperature is 13°C (55°F) and feed once a month. You cannot over-water the Cyperus; it is perhaps better to stand it in a deep saucer of water and keep topping up the saucer. Never totally immerse the pot as the stem of the Cyperus may rot.

Dizygotheca is a slender shrub with very attractive slender leaflets. On a young plant the leaves are copper and turn dark green as the plant ages. A minimum temperature of 13°C (55°F) is required together with a fairly humid atmosphere. The leaves enjoy being sprayed in high summer.

There are many types of **Ficus** of which the Rubber Plant is the most well known. The leaves are a dark leathery green carried on a single stem. The height can reach to 6ft or more. The new leaf emerges from a red protective sheath found at the tip of the stem. Water moderately but never allow the soil to dry out. Re-potting, if necessary, should be done in spring. Propagate by taking stem cuttings. The leaves will respond to treatment with leaf shiner occasionally, which will make them a

Left:
**The mature
Cyperus grown
from a cutting
similar to the one
illustrated in the
smaller pot**

Right:
**Fatsia well
displayed**

lovely dark green. The plant will withstand a minimum temperature of 18°C (65°F). Stand them on their own or put at the back of a display.

Bright light will keep **Fatsia** (Japanese Fatsia) short and sturdy although it likes other conditions as well. The plants can reach a height of 5ft in three years, so grow one in an area big enough to take it. It does not flower but has very attractive pale green leaves which grow as rosettes. The leaves are shiny and are incised with several lobes. They like cool temperatures and if the room is over 17°C (63°F) the leaves will become soft and thin, and liable to flop. Keep the humidity high by standing on wet pebbles. If kept reasonably cool the plant will withstand adverse conditions if the temperature drops suddenly and during the winter when the plant is resting a really cool temperature is best. Water plentifully to keep the compost moist and do not allow it to dry out otherwise the leaves will fall off. Re-pot as soon as the plant needs it and use a large pot of about 8–10in. To prevent this plant from taking over you can drastically prune it by up to half of its growth. Do this in the springtime and you will have a wonderful bushy specimen.

Fatshedera (the Ivy Tree) has thin erect stems that carry long-stalked leaves all along their lengths. They can grow to 4ft and need staking. It is possible to plant several plants in one pot to give a bushy effect. They are very easy to grow and will tolerate a wide range of temperatures and light

The ever-popular Monstera, one example showing an aerial root

Left:
The Maranta folds its leaves at night giving rise to its popular name, 'Prayer Plant'

conditions, although they do best in a reasonably bright light. The plant likes to rest in the winter so place it in a cool position of about 10°C (50°F). When resting it does not like to be too warm. Keep the humidity up by standing the plant on a tray of wet pebbles but water the plant moderately and when resting keep the compost fairly dry. It grows quite slowly so it does not need re-potting very often.

There are many varieties of **Hedera** (Ivy), which is a woody-stemmed climbing or trailing plant, with leaves of varying shades of green – from very dark to pale green with white giving a marbled effect. The leaves also have a leathery texture. The trails produce aerial roots and when they come in contact with a suitable damp surface will attach themselves to it. Hedera can tolerate a broad range of room temperatures, but prefers to be constant. The minimum temperature is 10°C (50°F). Propagate by taking tip cuttings.

A plant with scarlet flower bracts which remain an attraction for many weeks is the **Guzmania**. Appearing out of the bracts will be found small white or yellow flowers which are comparatively short-lived. They like a light airy compost which must be free of lime, so all peat-based types are suitable. The plant will thrive in high humidity and looks attractive stood on a tray of damp pebbles. Try to maintain an even temperature of 16°C (61°F) all year round. Propagate in spring by planting offsets (see page 31).

Maranta (Prayer Plant) is a low-growing plant and at most reaches a height of 6in. The leaves are longish, oval in shape, and pale green with what appear to be crack spots going up each side of the mid rib. The popular name of Prayer Plant derives from the plant's tendency to fold its leaves at night. Minimum temperature for the Maranta is 13°C (55°F); below this it will not thrive. Propagate in spring either by taking leaf cuttings or by division.

Monstera (the Swiss Cheese Plant) has large shiny leaves, that when mature develop holes and gashes. This is an easy plant to grow providing the winter temperature does not fall below 10°C (50°F)

and the plant is not subjected to draughts. Clay pots suit this plant best as it can become rather heavy, reaching a height of 6ft or more. Aerial roots are produced which can be left. Keep the compost evenly moist.

A popular indoor fern, the **Nephrolepis** has delicate green long arching fronds, each frond being divided into many narrow pinnae. Nephrolepis will grow actively all year given the right conditions. Slender furry runners grow out from the rhizome, putting down roots and produce new plants at their tips. Normal room temperatures can be tolerated throughout the year, minimum temperature 13°C (55°F). Never let the compost become dry. Re-pot in spring using half soil-based potting compost and half leaf mould. Propagate by potting the plantlets when required.

Peperomia has long slender flower spikes which look like mouse-tails! The leaves are dark green, velvet-textured and striking to look at.

The plants have a low habit but need a high humidity and warm temperatures, in winter not falling below 10°C (50°F). Keep the compost dry in the winter. Propagate from stem cuttings; leaf cuttings and leaf stalks (see page 45).

Philodendron (Sweetheart Vine) can climb or trail, reaching great heights and lengths. The leaves are dark green and can be long and pointed, sword-shaped, or heart-shaped.

The plants are easy to grow and very adaptable to all sorts of conditions. They need supports and stout sticks covered in moss are ideal for this. Repot when necessary into a peat-based compost. The plants can take pots of 8–10in diameter. They prefer a high humidity and like to have the leaves sprayed with water occasionally. Do not let the winter temperature fall below 10°C (50°F).

Creeping or upright-growing **Pilea** makes attractive foliage plants, although they can become straggly when old. The creeping types look very good in shallow pans or in the front of a bigger display, filling in the gaps. The temperature must not drop below 12°C (53°F), or the plant will die. Pilea must have a high humidity, but water them

Ficus: a new leaf will emerge from the red sheath at the tip of the stem

sparingly at all times. Propagate in the spring by taking tip cuttings.

A very popular houseplant, the **Saintpaulia** (African Violet) is much loved for its rich and colourful flowers, of which some are single and others multiple. The colours range from white, pale pink and variegated to the deep mauve which is well known. These flowers rise from the middle of the plant with the smallish velvety leaf around the edge. The African Violet likes high humidity and a minimum temperature of $13°C$ ($55°F$). Water moderately. For re-potting use lime-free or peat compost and propagate by taking leaf cuttings any time.

Sansevieria (Mother-in-law's Tongue) has striking upright foliage with green centres, edged with yellow. To keep producing more leaves the temperature should not fall below $15°C$ ($59°F$). They can survive short spells at $7°C$ ($45°F$). Water moderately, keeping the compost in the dry side. Many people kill these plants off by over-watering. Propagate by dividing side shoots. This plant will give height to flower displays but looks equally good on its own.

Saxifraga (Mother of Thousands) is very easy to grow and is most attractive. The adult produces quantities of young plants on stolons rather like strawberry runners. These runners hang from the main plant looking very pretty. Small white flowers appear on tall stems in the summer. The plant likes a wide range of temperature and can tolerate spells at $7°C$ ($45°F$). This plant is ideal for hanging containers.

Scindapus can climb or trail showing off its attractive streaked yellow and green leaves. The plants are easy to grow but be careful not to over-water which will make them straggly and the leaves turn brown. To promote a bushy growth prune back to one-third in the spring.

An average winter temperature of $10°C$ ($50°F$) is required to let the plant rest. Feed every three weeks during the growing season. Propagate by taking cuttings from the top of strong stems. To keep the variegated leaves make sure the plant gets

Left:
Peperomia beginning to show flower spikes

Right:
A Sansevieria which has produced two offsets; when re-potted these will produce two new plants

plenty of sunshine.

Schefflera (Umbrella Plant) has attractive delicate and glossy leaves which radiate from the stems to give the appearance of an umbrella. This plant is most useful for arrangements and also looks good on its own, for a well matured plant can attain the height of 6ft. Water moderately to keep compost moist all through the year with a minimum temperature of 13°C (55°F). Re-pot every other year.

Sinningia (Gloxinia) has fibrous-rooted tubers, and produces clusters of brightly coloured tube-like flowers. The leaves are fairly large, pale to dark green and are covered in fine hairs which makes them feel velvety to the touch. Gloxinias need a certain amount of humidity, but do not stand pots in water. The plants may be stood on a tray of moist pebbles during the growing season only. Feed every two weeks, but only when flowering has stopped, and stop feeding when top growth has died down. Propagate by taking either stem cuttings or leaf cuttings, or by growing from seed. Minimum temperature 16°C (61°F).

The **Stephanotis** has lovely white flowers which are sweetly scented. There are very few houseplants that give indoor fragrance and this is a must. The plant also has attractive evergreen leaves. The plant climbs and is best purchased when already mature, for your nurseryman will have trained it round all sorts of interesting supports.

A warm temperature must be maintained, at least 18°C (65°F). In the winter keep the plant at around 10°C (50°F) to enable it to rest. Re-pot in compost that is lime-free and water the plant with rainwater or distilled water. Syringe the leaves occasionally (see page 38). This is a difficult plant to keep but well worth the effort.

Tillandsia is interesting and a little unusual; its rosette of delicate leaves has a rich pink bract coming from the centre of the plant, which looks like the scales of a fish and is rather similar in shape. On the edge of the bract a bright violet-blue flower appears. Tillandsia grows actively all year

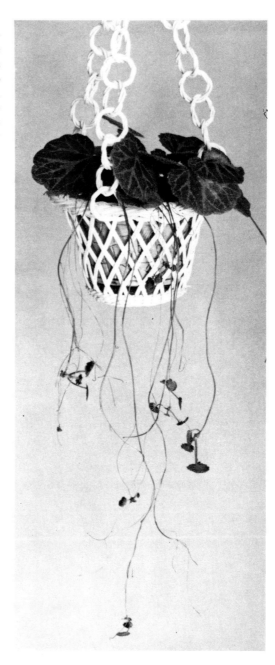

Left:
Saxifraga makes an ideal plant for a hanging basket

Right:
Scindapus

Left:
Schefflera makes a fine display plant and is very easy to grow

Right:
Tillandsia showing its fish-like flower bract

and likes a minimum temperature of 14°C (57°F). Feed once a month with half-strength liquid fertilizer. Propagate by taking offsets when they have attained a height of 3in. Tillandsias need very little water, but do like to be sprayed regularly.

Tradescantia (Wandering Jew) must be one of the easiest plants to grow, and is very popular. The leaves are variegated, long and pointed. The plant can be encouraged into a bushy form or allowed to trail. Tradescantias will survive in temperatures of 7°C (45°F) but to promote fast growth keep them at 17°C (63°F) or above. Do not allow the compost to dry out because the leaves will turn brown. Propagate by taking stem cuttings. This is so easy to grow that children can 'play' with it successfully.

Plants Tolerant of Shade

All houses have shady places that do not receive much light. It is possible to keep plants in these darkish areas, providing you choose those that do

The very easy-to-grow Tradescantia which is often used to introduce children to the hobby of houseplants not mind a little darkness in their lives. Plants left in these areas for any length of time do not require so much watering. Also, if the dark place happens to be cool as well, the compost will become cold if too wet and almost certainly kill the plant. What then can you use in the 'dark'? Of the plants already mentioned, the following do not mind having the 'lights' turned out for a little while. But do not abandon them for ever. Rescue them into the light occasionally to help increase growth and vigour.

Aspidistra	Monstera
Fatsia	Nephrolepis
Fatshedera	Philodendron
Ficus	Pilea
Hedera	Sansevieria
Maranta	Schefflera

Nephrolepis will enjoy a shady position

2 Care and Maintenance

After you have purchased your new plant from the nurseryman you have a duty to keep it in the pristine condition in which you received it. Left to its own devices the plant will suffer from neglect in a short space of time, and you will have a very sorry-looking specimen.

Plant care is not particularly difficult and when you have mastered a few simple rules you will be able to keep your charges in a beautiful and healthy state.

All plants must be kept in a well-drained pot. Plastic pots have drainage holes in the bottom to ensure adequate drainage, but clay pots must have in addition a layer of broken crocks placed in the bottom. Be very careful about watering. Over-watered plants will be more prone to diseases and poor growth. Under-watered plants will shrivel and possibly die. Do not water on the little-and-often principle; the water will not reach the bottom of the compost and thus the roots will not receive enough water. Give your plants a good drink to keep the compost evenly damp. In the active growing season and summer most plants will require more watering but in the dormant winter months they will need to be watered less often and in some cases hardly at all. Plants purchased from a reputable nursery will have a label advising on watering and other general care. Read this well and follow the instructions given.

Plants can become remarkably dusty and whereas furniture receives a frequent dust and polish, plants are often neglected. Leaves contain small pores that help the plant breathe. If these become clogged up with dust, the health of the plant will be affected. So keep the leaves clean. Wash smooth leaves frequently with tepid water and if the leaves are greasy, a small amount of soap in the water will not hurt the plant. Some varieties which have dark green leaves, such as the Rubber Plant, respond well to a proprietary leaf-shiner. This should only be given to plants that like it and then very sparingly. Do not apply in low temperatures. Plants with textured leaves or varieties which have an abundance of leaf hairs, e.g. the African Violet, should not be washed as this may damage them.

During the active growing season, your plants will have to be fed. Feeding will encourage new growth and healthy flowers. You can either feed them by diluting the feed in the water, and watering it in, or you can use foliar feed. The latter is diluted in water, sprayed onto the leaves and then absorbed through the leaf pores. Do not however spray the former type onto the leaves or stems as this will burn the plant. There are several brands of feed available and probably the best known is Baby Bio. It does not really matter which make you use provided you follow the instructions given on the bottle label.

If your plants are doing well, they will be growing quickly and the time will soon come when they need re-potting. Usually this needs to be done once a year. There are signs to look for if you suspect that a plant is 'pot-bound'. Roots will appear through the drainage holes, and leaves will start wilting very soon after watering because the compost does not hold the water. Older leaves will turn yellow and drop off and the younger leaves

Top left:
A plant in need of urgent attention: the leaves are turning brown, and left unattended this plant will die

Top right:
The roots protruding through the bottom of the pot are a sign the plant needs re-potting

Bottom left:
Turn the plant upside down and allow it to rest in the palm of your hand

Bottom right:
Re-plant in a pot the next size up surrounded by fresh compost and firm the plant in

will remain small. To examine the plant, turn the pot upside down, while holding the top in the palm of your hand with the stem between the middle two fingers. Tap the base of the pot with your other hand and gently ease the plant and root ball out of the pot. If the root ball consists of a mass of roots coiling around each other with very little soil in between then the plant is pot-bound.

When re-potting use a new pot which is the next size up from the old one. If too big a pot is used, the plants will feel lost and not grow as well. Also remember, if using a new clay pot, to soak this first, otherwise the pot will absorb too much water from the compost and the plant will be deprived. Use only the very best soil or compost. Do not use soil dug from the garden as it will contain all manner of pests and possible diseases. Composts are either soil-based, such as John Innes, or peat-based. They are sterile and correctly balanced for your plants. Suitable composts are available from all garden nurseries. Place enough compost into the bottom of the pot so that when placed inside the root ball is about an inch from the top of the pot. Position in the centre, then gently firm in more compost around and on top of the root ball. Tap the pot gently on the table so that the compost settles, then add more compost. Water well when finished. Place the plant in a shady place for a day or two so that it recovers easily. It should not be necessary to feed the plant for about six months as the new compost will have all the right ingredients but a highly vigorous, growing plant may need feeding inside three months.

Late spring is the best time to re-pot but it can be done at any time if by not re-potting the plant will suffer.

When observing your houseplants make a mental note of how they are doing. Remove any dead leaves and flower heads as soon as they appear. Watch to see if they become straggly, which could mean they are not getting enough light. It could also mean that they need pruning. If your house has undergone a dramatic temperature change, due to freak weather conditions or failure in the central heating system then keep a close eye on your plants. Any damage may not be apparent immediately.

When going on holiday, remember that your plants may be served a death sentence in your absence. If you intend to be away for several weeks, then you must find a 'plant-sitter' who will look after them. But a few days' absence need not result in dead plants on your return. The plants could be stood on wet sand: enough water will be drawn from the sand for the plants. Pinch out the flowers and buds, which will reduce the amount of water the plants will need. Remove all plants from the sun and for longer spells away pack them into a box filled with damp peat. There is capillary matting available which will seep a certain amount of water. If the pots are placed on this they will derive enough water. The matting can be left beneath a dripping tap, ensuring that it will not dry out; so the plants can be left thus for some time. Plants in a clay pot need a wick pushed through the drainage hole to connect with the matting or other water source.

Plants could be stood in the sink with about an inch of water in the bottom. Plants can be safely left in this way for about a week to ten days without any risk of damage to the roots by water. If the top of the sink is covered with polythene, a 'tent' will be formed which will also maintain the humidity. The bathroom, providing that there is enough light, is often an ideal place to leave plants when going away.

Maintaining the correct humidity is very important. Many species come from warm moist climates and require steady heat and ample moisture in the air. Putting several plants together in a group will help them generate their own local humid conditions by combining the vapour given off by the leaves in a restricted spot. With a single plant, try sitting the pot on a tray of pebbles which are kept wet, or place the pot inside a larger one which has been lined with damp peat. Special sprays and misting devices can also be purchased which will give a fine spray of water mist over the

Guzmania needs careful attention to produce best results

plants to humidify the air. Do not place the plants over a radiator. The atmosphere here will be so dry that the plant may literally shrivel to death.

Kept in the right conditions, your plants will enjoy a healthy existence but they may fall ill even though you are caring for them properly – and such problems are the subject of the next sections.

Pests

Ants
Ants get everywhere; they are a nuisance because they loosen the soil, but they also carry aphids from one plant to the next. Panant sprinkled lightly near the plants should solve the problem.

Aphids
Commonly known as greenfly, aphids spread very quickly from plant to plant and are at their worst in spring and summer. They will cluster on new shoots and the undersides of leaves causing the plant leaves to turn yellow and curl. The general growth becomes stunted and distorted. Aphids produce a honeydew which is a sticky substance on the leaves and stems. This will attract sooty mould, a fungal infection. Spray aphids with Malathion or Derris.

Leaf Miners
The adult fly does little damage; it is the maggot which hatches on the leaves and feeds on the tissue just below the surface. As the maggot moves a green wavy line will be seen across the leaf. Sometimes blisters also appear. Spray with Malathion.

Mealy Bugs
These are dark grey insects which produce blobs of white fluff. They collect in the joints of stems and on the undersides of leaves. The bugs can be scraped off with a knife, then the plant should be sprayed with Malathion once a week for three weeks. Alternatively, a cotton wool bud dipped in methylated spirits and wiped over the affected parts will be just as successful.

Red Spider Mite
These are very difficult to spot, so you will need a hand magnifier. The mites prefer hot dry conditions such as are found in centrally heated houses. Keeping the plant humid should discourage this pest.

The mites are pale yellow or red and round in shape. They suck up the sap, casting off their skins as they thrive. A matted webbing produced by the mites can be seen wrapped around the stems. Spray with Derris twice a week for three weeks.

Scale Insects
These look like immobile waxy deposits on the stems and leaves. Underneath the deposit the scale insects will be hatching out of the eggs and feeding off the plant's sap. As they mature they will move to a new area and produce another waxy shell in which to lay more eggs. A sticky honeydew is produced which can encourage sooty mould on the plant. The scales can be rubbed off with methylated spirits. Spray with Malathion.

Thrips
These are tiny black winged insects which will attack leaves and flowers producing white dots and streaks. Spray with Malathion.

White Fly
This pest is seen on the undersides of leaves. It is a tiny white moth-like fly. The larvae suck out sap, producing lots of honeydew which makes the leaves very messy. In severe attacks the plant may die. Treatment must include removal and burning of the infected parts. Spray the remainder with Bioresmethrin at four-day intervals. This will destroy the larvae. The adult fly will die naturally.

Diseases

Sooty Mould
The honeydew produced by several pests is an ideal growing medium for sooty mould. It is a black fungus which is best removed with a mild detergent.

Mildew
Powdery mildew looks like white dust, and downy mildew is fluffy. Poor air circulation can cause mildew. If an outbreak occurs, dust the plant with sulphur twice a week.

Fungal Spots
Humid conditions may cause and encourage fungal spots. They appear as circular soft brown patches on the leaves. Remove badly affected areas and spray once a week with Benomyl for three weeks.

Damping Off
Caused by unsterile soil, over-watering and cool moist conditions, this will rapidly kill a plant by rotting the roots and stem. Re-pot the plant and ensure that the conditions are not too wet and cold. Water the plant with Benomyl solution once every ten days for a month.

Botrytis
Commonly known as grey mould, the fungus will live on old leaves and stems and dead flowers. Untreated it will attack the rest of the plant. The first symptoms appear as brown patches on the leaves, which turn into a grey fluff. Remove the affected parts and spray Benomyl once a week for three weeks.

3 Propagation

Propagating your own plants will widen your hobby and provide you with an endless supply of 'free' specimens. Many species need sophisticated greenhouse facilities and constant monitoring but we are not concerned with those. The methods outlined here are those suitable for the kitchen windowsill or a spare corner of the living room.

Propagating plants is not difficult but each plant has a method that suits it best. You can choose from seed, cuttings, division or layering. Perhaps your only attempt at rearing young plants has been to dump a bit in a jamjar filled with water. This technique works reasonably well with some, notably the Busy Lizzie and the Spider Plant but it is far better to use the correct type of compost in a small pot. In any case pots will look neater dotted around the place than an odd assortment of jars and milk-bottles.

Growing from Seed

This is probably the slowest method but your patience will be well rewarded. Almost anything that flowers can be propagated this way. You will need to pick the seeds off the adult plant when they begin to dry and shrivel. Do not sow them immediately but wait until they have properly dried off. Keep them somewhere warm and dark during this time. It will usually take about a month before they are ready.

When ready to sow choose a correct type of compost such as John Innes special seed compost. Make sure that the pots or seed trays that you use are clean and have not been used for other sowings in the past. Moisten the compost first then press it

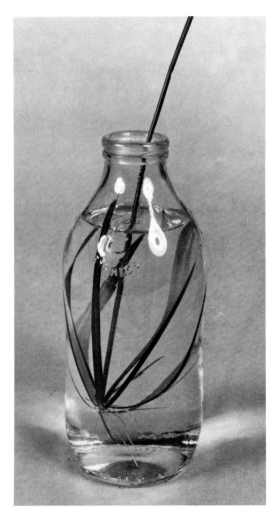

The Cyperus leaf can easily be propagated in water. Notice the extensive root system. This example is ready to be potted in a good compost

44

down gently into the seed tray so that the top is even. Spread the seed thinly on the top then cover lightly with a little fine moistened compost. Be careful not to overcrowd the seeds as they will all compete for nourishment and may also suffer from damping off. This complaint kills young seedlings and is caused by either overcrowding or too much watering. After sowing cover the tray or pot with a sheet of glass or polythene and put them somewhere safe but in a light position. Examine them frequently as some will start to germinate very quickly. They may need some water but attend to this very sparingly. Also be careful of watering from the top as a young seedling is easily knocked off course and damaged. Better to water from the bottom by allowing the tray to stand in some water.

Ensure that the seedlings are in a very light position otherwise they will grow long and straggly trying to reach the light. Seedlings that do this rarely make strong adult plants so if it begins to happen then move them quickly to a lighter home. Make sure that they are also out of draughts and try to maintain an even temperature whilst they are actively growing.

Plants that can be raised from seed include Coleus, Cyclamen, Fatsia, Schefflera, Solanum. Some plants can be grown from the stone or pip. The Persea (Avocado) is an example.

As your seedlings develop there will come a time when they will need pricking out into a larger pot. This will give them more space to develop and also give them an individual home. This is a delicate step as it is very easy to damage the young plant, so take your time. Prepare a new pot with John Innes No. 2, making sure that the soil is moist and well packed into the pot. Make a hole in the centre of the compost using a pencil or other round wooden stick. Make the hole quite deep. Next take the tray of seedlings, and place it on the table with some newspaper by the side. Carefully remove a seedling. Do not pull it out but remove some of the soil around the root ball as well. Next let the root and soil fall gently into the hole in the compost. When the seedling is in position, press the compost around it gently but firmly. The seedling may become limp for a while. There is no cause for concern as this is due to the shock it has had moving house. It will recover in a couple of hours or so, but keep the transplant away from the sun for a few hours.

One move of house may be enough for most young plants and it can stay in its new pot until an adult and ready for potting on when it gets pot bound.

Growing from Cuttings

The next method of propagating is to use cuttings. Cuttings can be taken from the stem, root or leaf but in the main it is the stem cutting which is the most popular. With most cuttings speed is of the essence although there are some exceptions to this rule. Usually the method is to remove the stem, a young shoot, that is not too young and delicate and not so old that it is hard and tough. Cut off a length of shoot about 4in long ensuring that there are at least three joints in the stem. Angle the cut to about $45°$ and dip this into a jar of rooting hormone (this can be obtained from any garden nursery). Then remove the last two leaves so that there is a reasonable length of stem before the leaves start. The cutting does not want too many leaves as it will have quite a struggle to root and extra leaves will require too much in the way of water supplies. Now place the end of the cutting into your pot and compost. This needs to be quite light: a mixture of peat, sand and Vermiculite will do nicely. Leave these in a light situation and again be careful about draughts. Do not over water but ensure that there is an adequate supply. The cuttings should root quite soon; some plants like the Busy Lizzie will root within seven days.

Others that you can take cuttings from include, Aphelandra, Begonia, Chrysanthemum, Fatshedera, Fatsia, Ficus, Hedera, Peperomia, Philodendron, Pilea, and Tradescantia.

Leaf cuttings are slightly different. Remove some leaves from the adult plant then cut a 2in triangle out of the underside of the leaf with the

Top left:
Cut a healthy side shoot near to the stem; angle your cut at 45°

Top right/bottom left:
Remove the pair of leaves nearest the cut

Bottom right:
Shorten the cut shoot about an inch below a node

Left, above:
Dip the fresh cut into some rooting hormone

Left, below:
Make a hole in fresh compost using a 'dibber' or pencil

Above:
Place the cutting into the hole and firm it in

main vein running through the middle and ending at the point. Then place the cutting point first into the compost. Cover this with a sheet of glass or polythene and leave for one or two weeks until the roots have begun. The Begonia takes well to this method of cutting although some plants, like the Mother-in-Law's Tongue, only need to have a piece of the leaf removed with a knife and then the area now exposed on the remainder of the leaf placed into the compost. This is very easy. The African

Violet does not even need to be cut with a knife! Just pull off a leaf together with the stalk and insert the end of the stalk into the compost. The Ficus (Rubber Plant) needs slightly more care and this is a case where speed is not of the essence. Strictly speaking it is a leaf bud cutting and a side branch will also need to be sacrificed in the process. But it is worth doing as Rubber Plants are very expensive. Cut off the leaf at the main stem with a sharp clean knife taking a piece of main stem with it.

Maranta is suitable for division. First remove the plant from its pot

Carefully break away the clumps of plant, without losing too much of the compost around the root ball

This picture shows the number of clumps obtained from the original plant. When re-potted each one will grow into a new individual

Leave the cutting for a little while to allow the sap to seal the cut surface. This will help to prevent the raw wound from being attacked by fungi. Place the cutting into a good potting compost and firm it in. Hopefully the area of stem included in the cutting will contain the beginnings of a leaf bud that will grow into the new plant.

Division

Propagating plants by division is really very easy. It is also essential because left undivided some plants will become overcrowded and may die off in the centre. Not all plants can be divided of course and some that will respond well to this type of treatment include Aspidistra, Asparagus Fern, Cyperus, Maranta, Sansevieria and Saintpaulia.

Saintpaulia (African Violet) is an easy plant to divide; just literally split the plant into two. Remove the plant and roots from the pot and feel around the base to find the clumps of root and

This picture shows the number of clumps obtained from the original plant. When re-potted each one will grow into a new individual

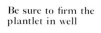

Chlorophytum
plantlet which has
been removed from
the runner and is
being potted to
grow into a new
plant

Left:
The African Violet
can readily be
propagated by
taking leaf cuttings

Be sure to firm the
plantlet in well

stem. Separated each of these clumps will produce another plant. Gently pull the clumps apart either with your fingers or using a sharp knife. Use a good compost like John Innes No. 2 to plant your new youngster.

Some plants have an underground stem called a rhizome. To propagate a rhizome, with a knife just remove a part that shows signs of sprouting and place this in a new pot.

Layering

The last method of propagation that we will mention is layering. Layering can be done either on the ground or in the air. It sounds complicated but really it is quite simple.

Chlorophytum can be ground-layered. They have plantlets which look very attractive on the adult plant but each of these can be propagated to form a new plant. They are attached to the parent by a dried stem called a runner. The runner can be cut leaving about half an inch still attached to the baby. Plant it into potting compost leaving the crown exposed. However, when the runner is cut in this way the baby will suffer from shock and will take longer to root. A better way is to leave the runner still attached to the adult plant. If the adult plant is put into the centre then the runners can be radiated out from it and the plantlets pegged into individual pots. A hairpin or staple will do. Cut the runners when the plantlets have rooted. Tradescantia can also be ground-layered.

Air-layering can be used to good effect with the Ficus (Rubber Plant) and the Monstera (Cheese Plant). The method will save a plant that has gone tall and straggly and lost its lower leaves. Choose a healthy part of the stem and remove a leaf about 8–10in below the growing tip of the plant. Here you make an upward cut in the stem with a sharp clean knife a little below the point where you removed the leaf, and where the new roots will grow. Make the incision just over an inch long and cut into the stem by about one-third. Put a sliver of wood such as a matchstick into it to keep it open and dust well with rooting hormone. Cover the incision well with moist sphagnum moss and tie this firmly into place. The plant will still derive the water and nourishment that it needs from the roots but any food that the leaves produce will remain in the top of the plant thus encouraging active new root growth at the site of the incision. Enclose the moss in a further wrapper to prevent dehydration and examine the moss frequently. Roots should appear within eight weeks. After that time remove the moss and cut through the stem below the incision and plant your new plant in good compost.

After-care

All of your new plants, whichever method you have used to propagate them, will need careful handling. Until established they will be more susceptible to disease and shock. Ensure that they are kept in an even temperature but not too hot; if anything err a little on the cool side and never put them in direct sunlight. Avoid draughts at all costs and fluctuating temperatures. Ensure that they have adequate nourishment from plant foods particularly while they are actively growing. They need considerable stamina to put down new roots. But make sure that any plant foods used do not touch the leaves or stem as they will be burnt and damaged. Foliar feeds are very good and easier to administer, but never give anything too strong as the plant may be killed off. Be careful about watering; do not get over-enthusiastic. Tender young roots are very prone to damage and they will easily rot. Over-watering will introduce wet conditions ideal for fungus growth and this may well mean the end of your new plant. Ensure adequate drainage in the pots by crocking them with pieces of old pots and keep the soil moist but not wet.

4 Design and Display

When you have brought your houseplant home, instead of just standing it in a drab plastic pot think about how you can display it more effectively.

Plant display can apply just as well to a single plant as to a group of plants. You can hang plants on the wall, or in free-hanging baskets, or in noble floor-standing arrangements. If you look around your house or flat there is usually somewhere in a room that would look perhaps more attractive with a small collection of plants. Remember of course that the plants must be suitable for the position you have in mind. You need not, however, be very 'artistic' to arrange plants, as they will almost do the arranging for you!

When planning arrangements, look at your existing houseplants, note their colours, leaf texture, and height, and whether the plants are prolific growers or slow-growing. Try mixing flowering types with green-leaf plants. These are just a few of the principles which will have become second nature to you now, having read and inwardly digested the earlier chapters of this book.

Now consider containers to put your plants in. There are lots of large and small pots etc. on the market, but, before you rush out to buy one have a good look around the house first. The kitchen is a good place for finding items that perhaps have not been used for months or even years. You may have an old copper pan that has been hidden away and just needs a clean – copper or brass 'set off' plants really well. On the other hand a pair of kitchen scales, such as the older type with weights, make an interesting and unusual 'container'. You may have one of the old cast-iron boiling pots, so have a good

forage and even pester Mums, Aunts and Uncles to see what they may have hidden away. Of course they may have decided to find containers for themselves, so keep looking, even pay your local 'junk' shop a visit and see what it has to offer in the way of pots and pans.

Garden centres have a vast array of houseplant receptacles in varying shapes and sizes, with facilities to hold one plant only, or more if need be. When buying from a 'centre' or shop, think carefully where this new item is going in your home, and consider its height and width. People have been known to fall in love with a container or stand, and on arriving home have been disappointed to find that the 'thing' will not fit into the desired place, or is out of keeping with the decor. Should your plants be in the conventional, now perhaps old-fashioned 'red' earthenware type of pot, which can look a bit dry and uninteresting, try brightening these up by using red Cardinal 'polish'. Give the pots a good clean first to get rid of the loose dust with a hard brush, and apply the polish as per instructions on the tin. This treatment is easy and cheap and the plant pots take on a new lease of life. We have not as yet thought of a way to deal with the standard plastic pots; they always look like plastic and most uninteresting, so we have found it best to cover or hide them in something that is more attractive, such as the decorative pot-holders readily available. Single plants of the trailing varieties, e.g., Campanula, will look very good mounted on the wall. Individual pots on the coffee table, for example, can have a bamboo frame attached so that climbing

54

types such as Hedera can be trained up the supports. Sticks covered in moss can be purchased from nurseries – they make ideal supports for taller plants such as Philodendron.

Hanging baskets are very popular but it can be difficult to maintain humidity round the plant, so choose the types of plant carefully. A good plant for 'hanging' is the Chlorophytum, which, when it gets its 'spiders', looks most graceful, especially in a more unusual container such as one of the 'rope' or bead baskets. The rope container lends itself to many plants; the Hedera likes to climb up the hanging supports, as do the Philodendron and Scindapus. The last-named, to climb the supports, needs the aid of green string or special clips, but be careful not to tie the plant too tight or you will cut off its 'circulation' and it will die off above the clip.

We have talked about only three plants suitable for the hanging container, but there are many others; try these easier ones first, then, when you are confident with your display and have got watering and care down to a fine art, branch out to the more difficult and perhaps more exotic. The best place of course to find these specimens is at your Garden Centre, but always adhere to the instructions given with your new purchase. Hanging plants need a little more watering than normal, but do not over-water.

Floor-standing displays can look very impressive although you do not need an army of plants to make them look beautiful. But before you decide to embark on a large floor display, look around your house first to make sure that you have room for one.

Floor-standing displays look effective in all types of large containers – circular, long, square, metal, wooden or plastic. The technique of making a semi-permanent display is as follows: Cover the base of the container with moist peat. Then place your plants (still in their original pots), angling them to give the effect required, in the main container. Ensure that the level of rims of the smaller pots is just below the surface-level of the display container. Fill around the pots firmly with

Chrysanthemums (left), available all year round, offer long-lasting colour to your displays, whereas the Cineraria (right) will give colourful impact in the spring

more moist peat until all the plants are secure. This technique will also enable you to change the display whenever you wish without disturbing all the plants.

Do not mix moisture-loving plants with those that require dry conditions. Maintaining the humidity should be easier than with single pots because the plants together will create a microclimate. Arrange the plants in order of height, with the taller ones to the rear and smaller ones at the front. Arrange trailing types near the edges so that they will trail downwards. Plants in flower can be situated wherever you wish to give the most pleasing effect.

It is possible to buy plants already arranged but it is much more fun to do it yourself. Try potting the following together – Ficus, Bilbergia, Cryptanthus and Peperomia; and Cyperus or Asparagus, Chlorophytum and Pilea. There really is no limit to what you can do or where to put them so let your imagination run riot!

Your Garden Centre will offer you a wide choice of plant pots, hanging baskets and floor-standing containers

An attractive arrangement of foliage and flowering plants

5 Bottle Gardens

Bottle gardens are enjoying renewed popularity. They are not a recent idea by any means. In Victorian times, for example, growing ferns in glass jars was commonplace.

Any deep glass receptacle can be used to make an indoor garden. Fish bowls, confectionary jars and the large carboys are all highly suitable, but avoid tinted glass as this restricts the light. The opening of the bottle, however, must be kept airtight. This will ensure that the moisture which comes from the plants will return to them. This continuous moisture given off, together with the light and the carbon dioxide gas given off by the plants, will keep the air inside the jar pure. In such an enclosed space, the soil could become insufficiently aerated. Because of this risk, when preparing your garden make the compost more gritty than usual by adding a handful of crushed charcoal to a peat-based compost. Alternatively, use two parts of John Innes No. 1 to one part peat and add a little crushed charcoal. Before you add the prepared compost to the bottle, ensure that the bottle is clean and dry. Add the compost through the neck of the bottle with a funnel. This will help to ensure that none of the compost sticks to the side of the glass. Let the compost settle to a depth of about four inches. Next moisten the compost thoroughly using a piece of hose which reaches down to the soil.

Planting your garden comes next. You will need some patience and care, so take your time. Firstly, tie a teaspoon to a strong stick. This will be used as a 'shovel'. A fork similarly treated can also be used. The stick must be longer than the depth of the bottle in order for you to manage your spade. Make shallow planting holes starting at the edge of the compost. Grip the plants with a piece of wire bent round the root ball and gently lower them into place, working from the outside inwards. Firm the compost each time before planting the next specimen.

When all the plants have been placed inside the bottle, cork it. The bottle may be left for several months before removing the cork to give a little fresh air. If necessary, give the plants a little feed and water using a long funnel to prevent fluid from splashing the plants.

Place the completed garden out of direct sunlight but in a light position, and turn it every day to give the plants even light. What plants can you grow in your bottle? Choose any moisture-loving species. Ferns and Bromeliads are suitable, but they could soon outgrow the space. If pruning becomes necessary use a pair of scissors. Most bottles will have a neck large enough for you to get your hand inside. Other possibilities include Saintpaulia, *Hedera helix* and Peperomias. In larger bottles try Dracaena, Chlorophytum and Ficus. Sansevieria and Pilea interspersed with the large plants will look lovely.

The garden will need very little attention when set up, but when some of the plants get too tall, remove them and re-plant with other miniatures.

Bottle gardens can be very attractive and great fun to arrange

Glossary

Active growth period: Period when plant
(growing season) puts out new leaves
and shoots.

Aerial roots: Roots that arise in
the air from stems.

Bract: Modified leaf which
often looks like a
flower.

Cutting: Piece of stem root or
leaf that will produce
a new individual.

Dormant period: Period when plant
will remain inactive
(normally winter)

Frond: Fern leaf.

Node: Point on a stem
where leaves and
side shoots arise.

Offset: A new plant
produced naturally
by the adult, usually
at its base. Offsets
are easily detached
for propagation.

Pinna: Single segment of a
leaf or frond.

Pinching-out: Removal of the
growing point of the
stem which
stimulates growth
further down.

Rhizome: Fleshy underground
stem.

Stolon: Shoot that creeps
along the ground
which roots and
produces new
plantlets.

The Cyclamen, one
of the most
popular
houseplants, given
the right conditions
and care will offer
an abundance of
colour

Index

Numbers in *italic* indicate pages on which illustrations appear